The Power of Ignorance
THE PLAY

TJ Dawe
and
Chris Gibbs

*Based on original material and characters
by Jeff Sumerel and Sam Reynolds*

© TJ Dawe and Chris Gibbs

All rights reserved. The use of any part of this publication reproduced, transmitted in any form or by any means, electronic, mechanical, recording or otherwise, or stored in a retrieval system, without the prior consent of the publisher is an infringement of the copyright law. In the case of photocopying or other reprographic copying of the material, a licence must be obtained from ACCESS the Canadian Reprography Collective before proceeding.

The Power of Ignorance name, characters, and original materials are the sole property of Spontaneous Productions, all rights reserved. For licensing agreements, more information and inquiries about The Power of Ignorance please visit www.powerofignorance.org or www.spontaneous.net or contact Vaguen@powerofignorance.org.

For more information on stage production rights visit www.tjdawe.com and www.chrisgibbs.ca.

Library and Archives Canada Cataloguing in Publication
Dawe, T. J. (Ti-Jon David), 1974-
The power of ignorance : the play / TJ Dawe and Chris Gibbs.

ISBN 1-897142-14-5

I. Gibbs, Chris, 1970- II. Title.

PS8557.A84697P69 2006   C812'.6   C2006-902674-2

Cover and interior photos: Mark Jackson, www.markjackson.ca

Canada Council   Conseil des Arts
for the Arts   du Canada

Brindle & Glass is pleased to thank the Canada Council for the Arts and the Alberta Foundation for the Arts for their contribution to our publishing program.

Brindle & Glass is committed to protecting the environment and to the responsible use of natural resources. This book is printed on 100% post-consumer recycled and ancient forest-friendly paper. For more information please visit www.oldgrowthfree.com.

Brindle & Glass Publishing
www.brindleandglass.com

1 2 3 4 5 09 08 07 06

PRINTED AND BOUND IN CANADA

What the critics have said about *The Power of Ignorance:*

This is the funniest piece I have ever seen at any of the 13 fringes I have attended. Heck, it's in the top five of the funniest plays I have seen in nearly half a century of theatre-going.

—montreal.com

An off-kilter, clever, absurd and howlingly funny script. Gibbs's delivery is a combination of dry wit and barely controlled madness that threatens to go off the rails at any time.

—CBC Edmonton

60 minutes of inspirational lunacy . . . painfully funny . . . the laughter carried on as people were leaving the venue.

—CBC Radio

[*The Power of Ignorance*] plunges to deeper levels of absurdity, dredging forth the bizarre as well as the disturbing. . . . Subtlety of writing and perfectly timed slapstick—*The Power of Ignorance* is brilliant comedy.

—*Uptown Magazine*

The Power of Ignorance is co-written by two Fringe favourites, TJ Dawe and Chris Gibbs (one-half of Hoopal). With this kind of pedigree you'd figure that this show couldn't go wrong . . . and you'd be absolutely right. . . . See it before it completely sells out.

—UMFM Winnipeg

A truly offbeat journey . . . [which] makes a compelling case for the old saw, ignorance is bliss.

—*Winnipeg Free Press*

For Jeff Sumerel and Sam Reynolds, who started it all.

The Power of Ignorance

Production History

The Power of Ignorance was first performed on June 13, 2003, at Theatre La Chappelle as part of the Garage International's contribution to the Montreal Fringe Festival. The technician was Josh Lamb. The festival was produced by Jeremy Hechtman and Patrick Goddard. The Garage International was administered by Shakti.

CAST

Vaguen: *Chris Gibbs*

Directed by TJ Dawe

Theme music composed and performed by Michael Rinaldi

The audience enters the theatre and sits down. They see the stage is set up with a small table, stage right. This table is covered with a black cloth, which reaches down to the floor. There is something on this table, also covered with a black cloth. A different black cloth.

It's unclear what this thing is. That's because it's covered with a black cloth.

The lights are dim.

Mystical, mysterious music plays.

When the time is right, the lights and music fade, gently, to darkness and silence.

There is a brief pause.

The same mystical, mysterious music starts up again.

From off-stage, we hear the sound of a man speaking into a microphone, and yet speaking as if to himself.

What he says is this:

> Duh . . .
>
> Duh . . .
>
> Duh . . .

The voice then speaks—again, into the microphone—but addressing the audience this time.

> Ladies and gentlemen, welcome.
>
> By attending tonight's seminar on "The Power of Ignorance," you have taken the first step on a journey.
>
> A journey of the mind.
>
> The journey will be exciting, strange, and frightening, and not everyone will make it.
>
> But you will not go alone.

> You will have a guide—a man who has shown countless before you how to tap into potential they never knew they had.
>
> A man named Vaguen.
>
> Vaguen has helped thousands of people in the tens of thousands of seminars he has given all over the world; speaking to successful people, wealthy people, good-looking people, and people just like you.
>
> Please put your hands together and welcome . . . VAGUEN!

The stage lights come up providing warm and generous illumination.

A man enters from offstage.

That man is Vaguen.

He wears black dress pants, a black suit jacket and a white turtleneck shirt, smartly tucked in.

He exudes confidence and charm.

He holds his fingers in a steeple position in front of him, which soothes the audience, whether they feel it or not.

The music fades out.

He speaks . . .

> Hello.
>
> My name is Vaguen.
>
> I'm here to talk to you about a philosophy that I believe will change your lives.
>
> A philosophy that I call . . .
>
> THE POWER OF IGNORANCE!
>
> I'd like to start by asking you a question.

> The question will be: "What is the most negative word in the English language?"
>
> Can anyone tell me the answer?

At this point, a brave audience member generally says "No."

> Well, I'll tell you, but I think you gave up very quickly.
>
> You'll kick yourselves, it's so easy.
>
> The most negative word in the English language is "No."
>
> And the opposite of negative . . .
>
> . . . is positive.
>
> And the opposite of "No" . . .
>
> . . . is "Don't know."

Vaguen nods smugly.

And so he should.

> I've dedicated years of my life to THE POWER OF IGNORANCE!
>
> I've travelled throughout the world, studying with Ig-masters, striving to pay little or no attention to what they told me.
>
> I have reached levels, where I never thought . . .

Once again, Vaguen nods smugly.

The audience thought he was going to finish the sentence, but he already had.

Or had he . . . ?

> . . . it would be possible.
>
> . . .to go.

. . . to.

Today I stand before you a Master Ignoramus.

From Ignorance comes Miracles.

From Ignorance comes Visions.

From Ignorance comes . . . Vaguen.

As he says his own name, he sweeps his hand into a V shape in front of his chest.

He looks down at his gesture, and then quietly remarks:

It's a V . . .

As you listen to me speak you may notice that my perception is very different from yours.

You will undoubtedly ask yourselves:

"What does this all mean?"

"Did he say what I think he said?"

"I don't understand!"

Well, if you don't understand, then you are already using your Power of Ignorance.

Yes, *your* Power of Ignorance.

From Ignorance comes Babies,

From Ignorance comes . . . who knows?

Are you confused?

GOOD!

Confusion is the Boulevard to Ignorance.

Walk down that boulevard now.

Make a commitment.

Join the few who understand

the importance of understanding

that a lack of understanding . . .

is unimportant.

You don't know what isn't possible.

Therefore, *anything* isn't possible.

Join me and give yourselves the benefit . . . of the *doubt*.

Vaguen walks over to the small table and takes a drink from a plastic cup of pure water. Once quenched, he replaces the cup, and then returns centre stage, to address the audience once more.

Now, Ignorance is nothing new.

Human beings have realized the value of Ignorance since before the first caveman fell down from the trees.

Into a cave.

Ignorance planted its seed in the fertile ground of the early human mind and has done nothing but grow.

We can find fragments of this Ignorance in philosophies from all over the world. Let us first consider . . .

He points to stage left.

. . . Western philosophy.

Millions and millions of years ago, in ancient Greece,

Socrates said "True wisdom lies in knowing what you don't know."

I couldn't have put it better myself.

Because I don't speak Greek.

Ralph Waldo Emerson said "To be great is to be misunderstood."

I don't know what he meant.

But he was a great man.

Jesus Humphrey Christ said "Father, forgive them, they know not what they do."

He gestures strangely to illustrate the term.

"know not" . . .

He shuffles his hands and gestures the other way.

. . . "not know"

Think about that.

Or don't!

All of Western civilization has been squirted from the loins of Ignorance.

He accompanies this last statement with a stubtle thrust of his hips and pumping of his fists.

And think about this.

All three of the great Ignorami I just mentioned came to glorious ends.

Socrates was forced to drink a cup of poisonous hemlocks.

Jesus was crossified.

And Ralph "Waldo" Emerson disappeared into a large crowd of people, and has never been seen again, despite his distinctive clothing.

Let us now turn from Western philosophy three hundred and sixty degrees and look at . . .

Vaguen indicates stage right

. . . Eastern philosophy.

The highest goal of Budd-Hism is to think about nothing.

Let me repeat that:

"Is to think about nothing."

"Nothing."

"No . . ."

". . . uhthing."

To achieve this, Budd-Hist sages have their apprentices ponder unanswerable questions like: "What is the sound of one hand clapping?"

Vaguen claps one-handedly, his single hand swinging through the air and making no sound whatsoever.

With the Power of Ignorance, every question is an unanswerable question.

The Power of Ignorance allows us to ask ourselves

"What is the sound of two hands clapping?" . . .

He claps two-handedly, but very quietly.

. . . and not even be able to venture a guess.

Vaguen turns toward his glass of water, but changes his mind and turns back to the audience.

Consider a dog.

Good.

Have you ever been playing a game of "Fetch-the-stick-and-bring-it-back-here" with a dog, and at one point tricked the dog by pretending to throw the stick, but actually hiding it behind your back?

Vaguen expertly mimes hiding a stick in his jacket's inner pocket.

And the dog tries to find the stick, but can't, and runs back with that confused look on his face.

Isn't that look adorable?

This time Vaguen actually does drink from his glass of water.

Now I'd like you to take a moment and imagine—in your minds—that you're sitting at home, minding your own business.

Suddenly the door bursts open and a man comes in, holding a gun.

He puts the gun against your head and says,

"Tell me, right now, without looking in an encyclopaedia, the name of the third president of G-hana.

"You have ten seconds.

"Ten.

"Nine.

"Eight.

"Seven.

"Six.

"Five.

"Four."

And we'll skip ahead to one, I think . . .

Vaguen bobs his head and mouths the words "Three . . . Two . . ." in a state of fierce concentration. Then . . .

"One!

"Time's up.

"Right. What's your answer?"

"I have no idea!"

There is the shortest of pauses . . .

"Good.

"If there's one thing I hate, it's a smarty-pants.

"If you had known the answer, I would have stabbed you.

"But now I won't."

Vaguen mimes stuffing the loaded gun into the front of his pants. Fortunately, it doesn't go off.

Now that probably just sounds to you like a fairy tale told to woo an over-thoughtful child to sleep, but no.

What I've just described is only one of literally nineteen situations in which Ignorance could actually save your life.

We've all read newspaper articles about people performing superhuman feats of strength while under extreme stress, such as lifting a car in order to save a child pinned underneath it.

Afterwards, when interviewed, those people would always say something like, "I just didn't think about it."

What does this tell us about the source of their strength?

In the heat of the moment they had forgotten that they could not lift a car . . .

Vaguen mimes lifting a car so large that it requires the use of an entire hand.

> . . . and so they could.

He effortlessly throws the car away.

> In a very real way, their Ignorance had saved that baby.

He now mimes picking up a tiny child between his thumb and forefinger.

He kisses that fortunate child and throws it away.

> Or perhaps some of you are familiar with how awareness of an injury increases the pain.
>
> Characters in movies often don't realize they've been shot until they look down and see the bloodstain.

Vaguen looks down at his shirt, and is reassured by its pure whiteness.

He looks back up at the audience.

> I'm okay.
>
> Cartoon characters will often run over the edge of a cliff and not fall . . . until they become aware that the ground is no longer beneath them.

As he says this he walks towards the edge of the stage.

> Who's to say what would have happened if they had kept their Ignorance intact?
>
> Perhaps even now they would be living happy fulfilled cartoon lives.
>
> But Ignorance doesn't just help fictional characters.
>
> I myself—Vaguen—have been helped by Ignorance in exactly this way.
>
> When I was twelve years old I broke my left arm playing soccer.

He holds up his right arm.

A few days later my mother reluctantly took me to the hospital where the doctor had to reset the bone before applying the cast.

She told me it would be less painful if I didn't see what she was doing, so I didn't look.

And I felt no pain at all.

None.

You see, it was my Ignorance, combined with the morphine, that saved me from excruciating agony.

Vaguen turns to get a drink, but as he remembers each of the following points he turns back to the audience.

Remember how tasty veal used to be before you knew where it came from?

Or hot dogs, before you saw the people who prepare them.

Or what about peaches!

I still remember when my mother told me the truth about peaches.

I didn't sleep for a week.

He takes a drink of water, visibly shaken.

Those poor, poor children.

Remember when you were a child and it was Christmastime and your presents would be wrapped up and waiting under the tree?

And every day seemed like a month.

And every month seemed like a whole day.

And you were so excited.

You didn't know what was inside that brightly coloured paper.

And you'd ask your parents and they'd say,

"Wait and see."

"Oh come on, please!!!"

"Well okay, it's a . . . oh no you don't! You nearly got me, you little scamp."

In character he rapidly gets very angry, raising a hand for a firm backhand blow.

Remember that?

And remember the ecstasy and anticipation of what was in there?

It was your Ignorance that gave you the most happiness.

Wondering what was in the presents was even better than opening them and getting a bag of cabbages, or half a pack of pencils, or a box of magic dirt.

Even a present you liked, and were allowed to keep, like the magic dirt, was more fun because of the anticipation of the day when it would turn into a puppy like your parents had promised you it would.

Waking each morning for three months and wondering—or . . . not knowing—if today was the day was much better than when the dirt, finally, was taken away by your parents who said "I guess you just didn't want it to turn into a puppy badly enough."

Wasn't it, though?

Or how about when you went to see a magician who did tricks—magic tricks.

He mimes a magic hand swirl, frightening himself.

Or perhaps he mimes an animal exhibiting its prominent claws.

Wasn't it better when you didn't know how the tricks worked?

Didn't you somehow prefer life when you had no idea where the rabbit went when the magician made him disappear into his scary top hat?

Wasn't that better than when your parents told you how it worked, about how the rabbit was sliced into tiny pieces at the bottom of the hat and its soul went to Rabbit Hell, where it had to dance naked in front of a big fat rabbit with no hair, until it was dropped into a pit where it was eaten by a giant little boy who was too much of a smarty-pants and deserved a good smacking with a wooden spoon!!

He calms down.

Ignorance is what made all our childhoods happy.

Vaguen walks to the glass but decides not to drink it.

I'm not thirsty.

Now, up until now I've been describing ways in which Ignorance has already enhanced your lives—in the past.

And in a moment I'm going to show you some ways in which Ignorance can help you that you may never have thought of—in the future.

But first I'd like to draw your attention to the fact that Ignorance is helping all of you right now.

In fact I don't think I'd be exaggerating if I were to say that without Ignorance, everyone in this room . . . WOULD BE DEAD!!!!

There is a terrifying pause.

Please, please calm down.

I didn't mean to alarm you.

Let me explain.

I think I can say—without fear of contradinction—that you are all breathing.

I think I can also say—also without fear of contradinction—that at least 75% of you have not been actively thinking about your breathing the entire time you've been here.

And yet not a single one of you has asphynxiated or fainted.

Remarkable, isn't it.

Yes it is.

Breathing—the very . . . water of life—has been in the hands of your inner Ignorance this whole time, and has been doing just fine.

And here's the truly saline point: if you were to actively pay attention to your breathing it would be substantially less effective.

It might even stop altogether.

You're thinking about your breathing now, aren't you?

Careful.

Unfortunately, by drawing your attention to this phenomnymum, I have placed your breathing under your conscious control, endangering all of your lives.

I apologize. It seemed important.

At this point Vaguen performs a series of boy-band dance steps.

Once he has finished and the audience has recovered, he speaks again:

I just performed a short sequence of boy-band-esque dance steps.

I did this to distract your attention from thinking about your breathing, thus allowing you to breathe Ignorantly once again, averting a mass death by suffocation, and saving all of your lives.

You're welcome.

This is just one of the many tools and techniques that we Igmasters can use to return ourselves and others to a state of healthy Ignorance.

How it worked was, for those few brief seconds, you stopped thinking

"Inhale, Outhale"

He inhales and he outhales after each respective word.

And instead you thought "Yum yum."

Unfortunately, by explaining the technique to you, I have returned the topic of conversation to breathing, placing you all back in jeopardy.

If I have to use the technique a second time, I won't explain why.

He performs another series of boy-band dance steps—different than the first series, but just as impressive.

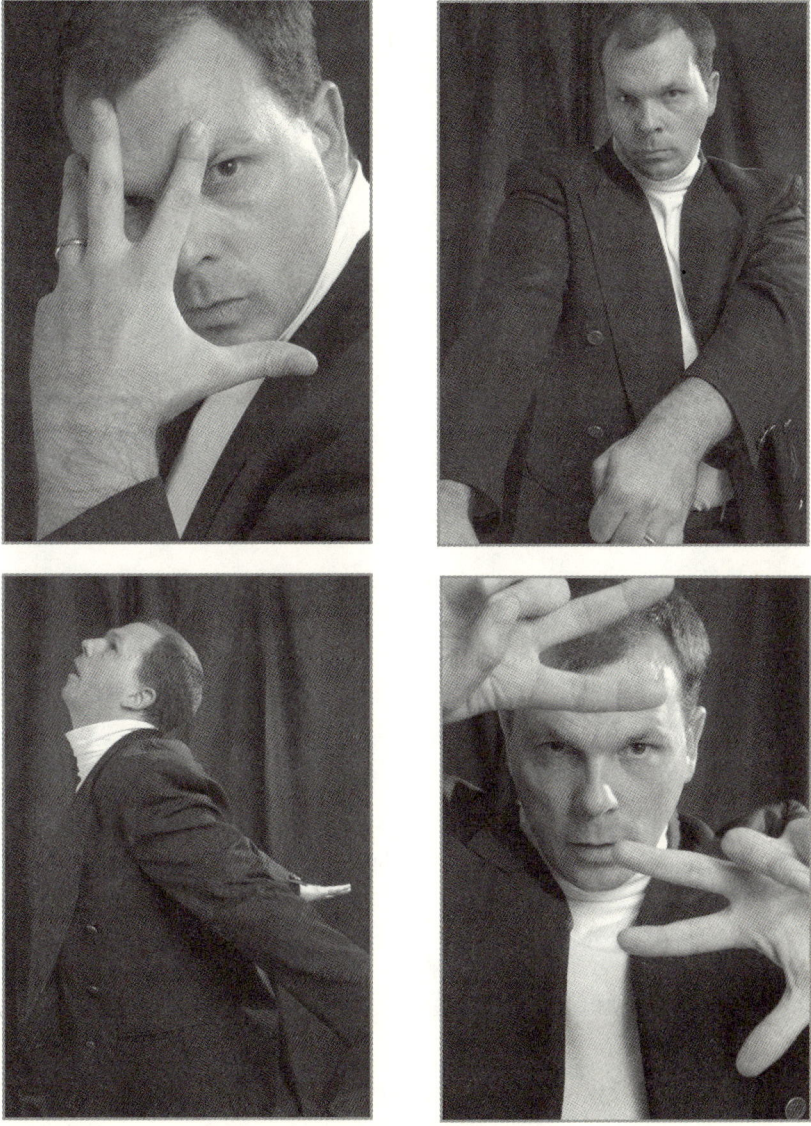

> I just performed that series of boy-band dance moves for no reason whatsoever.

Vaguen winks at the audience broadly.

Savouring the triumph of this last point he so successfully made, he walks over to his glass.

He then dips a finger in the water and licks it.

> Let us look now at just a few examples of how the Power of Ignorance can push us further in all areas of our lives.
>
> We'll start by imagining . . . a human brain.

Vaguen mimes holding a human brain, a full two inches in diameter.

> The human brain is a complex mass of energy, most of which is neglected.
>
> Yes.
>
> Neglected . . .

He mimes throwing the brain over his shoulder and almost catching it.

> Do you know how much of the brain isn't ever used?

He turns and picks it up off the floor, brushes off a hair, then throws the brain offstage.

> Ninety per cent.
>
> Isn't that astonishing?
>
> Yes it is.

He wipes his hands on the curtains.

> How can I bring home ninety percent to you?
>
> Perhaps if you thought of it as almost eleven twelfths.

He sniffs his fingers and then washes them in the glass of water.

> Or imagine that you're from a family of ten siblings, and the other nine didn't show up at your birthday party.
>
> Ninety per cent . . .
>
> Picture a glass of water.
>
> I know what you're doing.

Vaguen stands in front of his own actual glass of water.

> No cheating.
>
> Picture a glass of water.
>
> Now . . . drink one tenths of it.
>
> You see in your mind's eyes how much is left?
>
> That's the amount of water the brain never uses.
>
> It really does boggle the mind.
>
> Ten per cent of it, at least!!

Vaguen laughs heartily at his own joke, but suddenly stops.

> The only people who use one hundred per cent of the human brain are cannibals.
>
> When my anthropologist friend first told me this, like you, I was confused.
>
> Then I used my Power of Ignorance, walked down that Boulevard of Confusion, and I realized, of course—cannibals would have to develop the use of more of their brains because they have to outwit other humans, in order to eat them.
>
> My anthropologist friend said "No! It's because they eat human brains!"

Yes! So therefore they have to remember more recipes, to make those yucky crumbly brains palatable.

At this my anthropologist friend threw up his hands in despair and left, obviously disappointed that I, by using my Power of Ignorance, had solved a scientific conundrum that had doubtless stumped he and his colleagues for decades.

Remember the most famous cannibal of all, Hannibal Smith.

He'd never have got Murdock, Face and Mr. T. to go along with his crazy schemes unless he was using the full hundred.

Vaguen taps his temple three times as he makes this point, and on the third tap accidentally pokes himself in the eye.

Freud divided the mind into three parts: the ego, the superego and the id.

Vaguen gestures for each word, indicating the id with a tickling motion.

But what of the remaining ninety per cent—this vast font of Ignorance?

We Igmasters call it the "Ig."

The Power of Ignorance will allow you to tap into your Ig.

Because after all, any fool can see it's better to rely on the ninety per cent that's not doing anything than the ten per cent that's already busy.

Vaguen walks to the glass, drinks from it, realizes it tastes awful, and swaps it for another one from behind the table.

Let us now turn from the human brain to the world of science.

Science and Ignorance are generally thought not to mix, but they do.

Remember the Hindenburg uncertainty principle?

"Is it helium or hydrogen?

I don't know.

Light a match.

If it doesn't burn, it must be helium."

The uncertainty principle teaches us that there must be limits to our knowledge, because sometimes by trying to observe a thing, to know it, we change it.

Unless it's helium.

But that notwithstanding, when we think of scientists, we think of people who aren't Ignorant.

We think of them as people who know things.

But science is not the same as knowledge.

All science is just a set of theories—or guesses—that suit the facts.

And scientific theories don't last forever.

They exist for a while, then are disproven, and replaced with other theories.

These too will then exist, be disproven and replaced, and so on.

Hundreds of years ago, in the past, scientific theories would last for hundreds of years before they were disproven.

Nowadays, theories will last just a few decades, perhaps even years.

And hundreds of years from now, in the future, scientific theories will last only a few months, or weeks.

And as science progresses, scientific theories will be disproven faster and faster. Eventually within days, then hours.

Scientists who have used the Power of Ignorance have reached this advanced stage already.

Many of them have produced theories that have been disproven within seconds, often as soon as they show their work to another human being.

Once by one of the very worms they were experimenting on.

Once by one of the very children they were experimenting on . . .

I'd like now, to look at how the Power of Ignorance can enhance our ability to deal with those around us.

I'm going to demonstrate a common technique used to enhance one's interpersonal skills.

Vaguen approaches the edge of the stage, and directly addresses a nearby audience member.

You sir, what's your name?

The man calls back his name.

Let's say "Steve" in this instance.

Hello there, Steve. It's certainly a pleasure to meet you, Steve. Tell me Steve, what do you do for a living, Steve?

STEVE: I'm an accounta—

By using Steve's name four times within the first thirty seconds of meeting him I have increased the chances that I will remember his name.

Now let's see what happens when we apply the Power of Ignorance to this technique.

Do you mind if I borrow you again Stan?

Hello there. What's your name?

The man tells Vaguen his name again.

For some reason he has changed it to "Steve."

Steve, Steve, Steve, Steve. Steve. Steve. Steve? Steve! Steve. Steve. Steve. Steve. Steve. Steve . . . Steve. Steve. Steve! Steve. Steve. Steve. Steve. Steve. Steve? Steve. Steve-Steve-Steve-Steve-Steve! Steve. Steve. Steve. Steve. Steve. Steve. Steve! Steve. Steve! Steve. Steve. Steve. Steve . . . Steve . . . Steve.

My name is Vaguen.

By using Steve's name forty times within the first thirty seconds of meeting him I have guaranteed that *he* will remember *my* name.

Probably the most famous example of the Power of Ignorance is the Wright Brothers.

Now, I know what you're thinking,

"Hey leave those groovy Wright brothers alone man! If it wasn't for them it would have taken you longer to get here!"

Please let me explain.

At the end of the eighteenth century, scientists all over the world were racing to be the first to discover the secret of Heavier Than Air Flight.

Many of those scientists had vast budgets, armies of researchers and huge resources at their disposal.

The Wright Brothers had none of this. They were just two bicycle repairmen from near Canada.

But what they did have was Ignorance.

You see, the first thing the brothers did when they began their work was to throw out all the existing research and knowledge on how flight would be achieved; thus proceeding from a position of Ignorance.

And as we know they succeeded in achieving Heavier Than Air Flight, while their better-funded, more established contemporaries were, quite literally, not achieving it.

That's a pretty inspiring true story of the Power of Ignorance.

But I prefer this story:

When Wilbur Wright was just fourteen years old, he sustained terrible head injuries in an accident while playing an early primitive form of ice hockey.

The doctors told his parents that based on their knowledge and experience, they knew that Wilbur would never recover, that he would never again read, write or think, and that any attempt to rehabilitate him would actually make things worse.

His parents decided to ignore this knowledge, and proceed from a position of Ignorance, and Wilbur, as we know, wasn't just rehabilitated, he went on to become one of the most important scientific minds of his or any other century.

Now that is a very inspiring story of the Power of Ignorance.

It's also . . . a lie.

But think about it. Wasn't it more inspiring when you didn't know it was a lie?

Just think what you could have achieved if you had had the fictitious Wilbur Wright as a role model.

You could have done anything.

"If Wilbur Wright could recover from his head injuries," you would say, "surely I can overcome my fears and program this VCR and go out and see some live entertainment!"

You can find this and many other untrue inspiring stories in my book "Chicken Soup for the Ignorant Soul"—available from Campbell's.*

---

* Now sadly out of print. For true inspiring stories, though, see *The Power of Ignorance, or Fourteen Steps To Using Your Ignorance To Become Happier, Safer, More Confident And More Likeable, To Forget Your Limitations, Inspire Yourself With Successes You've Never Had And Achieve Your Goals In Addition To Enhancing Your Ignorance To Promote All Those Things And Well-Being Generally*, from Brindle & Glass.

But why just be inspired by the achievements of others?

It's so much more powerful when you can be inspired by the achievements of . . . yourself.

People who have overcome incredible odds will often say that afterwards everything else seemed easy.

"I climbed Mount Everest," they would say. "Surely I can change the ink in this printer!"

But you don't have to climb Mount Everest to benefit from this.

All you need to do is forget the knowledge that you never have.

The next time you find yourself in a difficult situation, simply say,

"Aren't I the same person who crash-landed in that plane and had to crawl twenty miles through jungle clutching my own severed head? Surely I can peel this orange even though I've just clipped my fingernails!"

"Hey! Didn't I program that VCR and go see that show that time? Well surely I can perform this triple-bypass surgery."

Ignorance is a key part of any success story.

Successful people when asked will always say things like,

"I don't know the meaning of the word 'quit'"

Or "I don't know what fear is"

Or "The words 'I can't do this' aren't in my dictionary."

By using the Power of Ignorance, you too can expand your lack of knowledge of the vocabulary of failure.

Just think what you could achieve if you didn't know the meaning of the words "quit," "fail," "stop that," "it's illegal you know" and "if it didn't work the last nineteen times, and you haven't changed anything, it's not going to work this time."

> Why, if I hadn't rid myself of the knowledge of the meaning of the words "Your philosophy is absurd and you'll never be a successful motivational speaker," I wouldn't be standing here today talking to this packed five-thousand-seat auditorium.

Vaguen walks over to the table and picks up his glass of water, but doesn't drink it yet.

> Now, a lot of times in our lifes, we find ourselves ahemmed in,

Vaguen's words are so important that he cannot take the time to stop talking to drink. He boldly drinks as he speaks. On the word 'ahemmed' the water splashes out of the glass, a distraction that would floor a lesser man, but Vaguen's concentration is rock-steady. (Not rock as in 'to rock the boat', which would suggest that it wasn't steady, rock as in 'a chunk of rock'.)

He continues speaking, undistracted.

> . . . constrained by what we tell ourselves we can't do.

> You know what I'm talking about—those moments when you suddenly find yourself . . . "Knowing too much"?

> When you catch yourself saying

> "I know this won't work."

> "I know they won't accept me."

> "I know I'm just a fake."

> "A big fat British fake."

Vaguen is somewhat affected by this last statement, and quietly closes his jacket over his fatness.

> These awkward moments of self-realization can be very damaging indeed.

> They can undo in seconds what has been built up by years of good luck, hard work and a pig-headed refusal to see your own shortcomings.

But thanks to the Power of Ignorance, there is a method available to bat away that awkward self-knowledge.

I'm talking about the Power of Ignorance Mantra.

By using the Igmantra you can silence that voice in your head that tells you what you can't do.

Then all of us can be as daring as Hindenburg or as successful as Andie MacDowell.

When these crises of confidence occur, stop and focus.

Focus on what is known as "middle air."

Vaguen mimes rubbing his tummy and patting his head.

Focus and breathe—without thinking.

Vaguen does a quick arm wave—popping and locking his joints—to prevent the audience from thinking about their breathing, thus saving their lives again.

Feel the Igmantra seep up through you, pushing up through your head, carrying all knowledge with it.

He says the following word with emphasis and deep meaning:

Duh . . .

Duh . . .

I'm a fake, Duh, I'm okay.

Try it with me.

Duh . . .

Vaguen attempts to lead the audience in the Igmantra, but the simple though slightly irregular rhythm of his pacing throws them off.

Duh . . .

Duh . . .

Don't worry about the timing, you'll get it eventually.

Use the Igmantra wherever you need it.

Perhaps at work while dealing with a difficult customer.

Or later on in a disciplinary meeting with your boss.

Or the next day at a very important job interview.

In your personal life, you can use the Igmantra while in the middle of a difficult conversation with a significant other with whom you intend to spend the rest of your life.

"I don't want to be with you any more."

"DUH"

"I mean it, I'm calling the police."

"DUH"

"You're coming with us."

"DUH"

"How do you plead?"

"DUH"

"Mr. Vaguen, if you do not answer the next question appropriately, you will be subject to a psychiatric evaluation."

"DUH"

"You again!"

"DUH"

"You're not getting away this time."

With sly confidence:

> "DUH?"

But most importantly, use the Igmantra in public.

Yes, in public.

I know what you're thinking.

"But people will stare at me! They'll be confused!"

Yes they will.

And what a warm feeling that will give you, to see their confusion, knowing that you have helped them tap into their Power of Ignorance.

Because as we know, confusion is the Boulevard to Ignorance.

Vaguen drinks from his glass once again.

I've been talking for some time now about the ways in which Ignorance can help you.

I think it's time for a quite dramatic demonstration.

One of the wonderful things about the Power of Ignorance is that it can be proven.

It doesn't have to be taken on faith, like positive thinking, gravity or penicillin.

Vaguen turns to the side, drawing up purpose and concentration.

He repeats the Igmantra to himself:

> Duh . . .
>
> Duh . . .
>
> Duh . . .

He then does a perfect handspring.

The audience gasps, and then applauds. Vaguen looks confused at the applause.

What's that strange slapping sound?

I have no idea.

What you just saw was . . . amazing.

To recap, I just performed a complete backwards somersault, leaping high into the air, then rotating a full three hundred and fifty degrees before landing back on my feet with roughly the same amount of noise as that made by a particularly agile cat.

Any of you faced with this task would say "I know I can't do that. I know it's too difficult,"

While I know no such thing.

I was able to perform that incredible acrobatic feat because I used the Igmantra to rid myself of the knowledge of the meaning of the words

"You have no acrobatic training."

"You haven't warmed up."

And "Let's face it; you're at least 60 pounds overweight."

Vaguen then picks up his glass of water.

I'm going to demonstrate this again, but this time with a double somersault, while holding this glass, without spilling a drop.

He executes another handspring, though crushing the glass and splashing water all over himself.

For a moment Vaguen's cool confidence has slipped, he looks embarrassed at the crushed plastic glass and the water on the stage and on himself.

Duh . . .

Duh . . .

The Igmaster reaches behind his table and swaps his crushed and empty glass for an intact one that is full.

Duh . . .

I think you'll agree that was another completely successful demonstration of The Power of Ignorance.

Now I'm sure you're all eager to try this.

And I urge you to do so.

I can see no reason why you shouldn't.

If you do try it, and hurt yourself, remember,

I don't know you.

The road to Ignorance is a long one.

It will take many years for you to achieve the levels of Ignorance that I have.

But there are shortcuts.

One that you might want to try is liquid Ignorance, commonly known as alcohol.

I particularly recommend a cocktail I designed myself, called the Ig.

It consists of vodka . . .

Vaguen drinks from his clear plastic glass full of clear liquid.

We're now going to take a short break.

You might want to take this time to experiment with what you've learned so far.

I believe there will also be liquid Ignorance available to you in the bar.

I thank you for your time so far, and I look forward to seeing you again in fifteen minutes.

*The stage lights fade out very slowly. * (see alternate middle)*

The audience applauds rapturously.

House lights come up.

Mystical, mysterious music plays.

As people get up to go to the lobby, some of them notice that Vaguen is still standing on stage.

He stands there, with his fingers in a steeple position for the length of the intermission.

He wears a practised smile all the while.

---

*Alternate middle

As the audience applauds, Vaguen runs confidently to the curtain, but, unable to find a way offstage, is forced to run across, his hand covering his face.

Intermission

From offstage a voice can be heard, speaking near a microphone. The voice is familiar, yet different. It sounds like how Vaguen might sound if The Power of Ignorance did not endow him with superhuman confidence.

> I can't go out there! They can tell I'm a fake. They know!

> Duh.

> Duh.

> Duh.

The stranger's voice is replaced by the silky reassuring tones of Vaguen, Igmaster.

> Ladies and gentlemen, welcome back.

> And thanks for coming back.

> Please put your hands together, making whatever sound that makes, for Vaguen!

Stage lights come back up and Vaguen returns to the stage to resume his seminar.

Once the intermission is finished the music and lights fade out.

Stage lights come back up and Vaguen resumes his seminar.

> Hello again.

> I'd like to begin this second half of our seminar by asking you a few rhetorical questions, for which, and I cannot stress this enough, no

verbal answers are needed.

How many rivers in Portugal begin with the letter "C"?

What's the Sanskrit word for "bashful"?

Where does "leather" come from?

You don't know, do you?

No one does.

We could spend years trying to find the answers to these and literally hundreds of questions just like them, and we'd wind up with nothing but a few dozen answers.

Or we could go the other way entirely.

The real key to being absolutely Ignorant is to rid yourself of all knowledge, and the first step to doing that is to acknowledge that knowledge is bad.

This "lacknowledgement" is easier than you think.

We all know that a little knowledge is a dangerous thing, so obviously a lot of knowledge would be even more dangerous.

Consider a dog.

A different dog.

Now a dog understands certain simple things, like hunger or territory, or 'who's my little snuffly-woo yes you are.'

But more complex matters like mathematic or board-games would be ununderstandable to even the smartest *German* Shepherd.

Try explaining Monopoly to your dog.

Imagine you had a lot of free time on your hands.

Try to picture a scenario in which something about you kept people at a distance and you found it difficult to make friends, or even acquaintances.

And you spent most of your time sitting around in your underwear.

No matter how much patience you had with your dog,

no matter how great your skills as a teacher,

no matter how clear, simple and direct your language,

at best that dog would be a mediocre Monopolist.

And believe me: you'd get pretty tired of beating him nearly three games out of four.

But more importantly, what would he do with this knowledge?

Could he play Monopoly with other dogs when you weren't there?

Would he ever stop trying to build houses on the railroads?

Or peeing on Free Parking?

Would he feel more like a "good boy"?

Would he ever choose any Monopoly piece other than the dog?

Or occasionally the old boot?

No he doesn't.

Wouldn't.

It makes you think.

What are the Monopoly games in our lives?

Other than Monopoly.

In what ways are we being mediocre human beings, when we could

be good dogs?

Vaguen runs his fingertip along the edge of the glass, causing it to sing preternaturally.

He then picks up three children's blocks—the kind with a single letter on each side. Or perhaps a number.

> These were my favourite toy as a child.

He stacks them on top of each other, and continues stacking them, removing the bottom one to take the summit point.

> "I'm going to build the highest tower anyone's ever seen and then I'm going to jump off and I'll die and everyone who was ever mean to me will be really sorry."
>
> I think we've all played that game . . .

Vaguen continues stacking the blocks, and then stops.

> I haven't done this since I was a child.
>
> So often people say that.
>
> "I haven't done this since I was a child."
>
> Why?
>
> Why do we lose our belief in disbelief?
>
> Why do we become bound by the constraints of common reality?
>
> Why have our building blocks been replaced with mental blocks?
>
> Why do our brain cells become prison cells?
>
> Why do our IQs become Haikus?
>
> Think about that one.
>
> It is very clever, and it does make sense.

Each of them is restrictive: mental block, brain cell, and the haiku is the most restrictive form of poetry, seventeen syllables.

Give a child a broken toaster and that child's imagination can make that broken toaster into anything.

Vaguen illustrates the term "broken toaster" by picking up and holding an actual broken toaster from behind his table.

A child might imagine this broken toaster to be . . . a wizard's toaster,

or a dragon's toaster,

or even a Swedish person's toaster.

Now, I know what you're thinking.

"Why would a wizard need a toaster? Surely they make toast by magic!"; "Dragons breathe fire!"; "Sweden's near Norway!"

Vaguen laughs.

Well, you've just proved my point.

Give that same broken toaster to an adult and they will ask "Is it still under warranty?"

Sad, isn't it?

Yes, it is.

Another adult might say "What do I want with a broken toaster?"

I know for a fact that one adult would say "Oh look what you've done, you've broken mummy's lovely toaster, you naughty naughty little brat! Go back to the cellar before I hit you with the wooden spoon again!! Hsssssss!!!!!"

"No, mummy, no!"

"Don't you 'no' me."

"Yes . . . yes I do—you're Mummy."

"Ooooooh, who's a little smarty-pants? We'll burn the pants off you then with this spoon!"

"Whoooooo-ooooooo!!!"

"Not so clever now, are you?"

"No! I'll never be clever again . . . never be clever again . . . never be clever again . . ."

Vaguen is somewhat discombobulated at this point.

He breathes heavily.

> Duh . . .
>
> Duh . . .
>
> Duh . . .

He seems to have recovered, and continues.

> When a child wants to play at being . . . a doctor for instance, he will go ahead and be a doctor.
>
> He doesn't enrol in imaginary medical school first; he doesn't buy fantasy text books or a dream white coat.
>
> He simply plays doctor.
>
> Imagine how different our world could be if adults did the same thing.
>
> Why can't any, or even all of us, simply start playing doctor right here and now?
>
> A year ago, a young man who had attended one of my seminars approached me and told me how much trouble he was having in medical school.

"Please," he implored me "being a doctor is my life's dream. How could I have known it would be hard? Tell me how the Power of Ignorance can get me through Med school."

"Well," said I, "medical science is all about Ignorance.

Think of the thousands of biological processes which occur within the human body every week without any of us being aware of them.

Think of how many seriously ill people are deliberately kept in the dark about how hopeless their situations really are, thereby sparing them and their doctors undue awkwardness.

Think of the high salaries doctors can charge because no one knows that nurses do all the work.

Think of the millions successfully treated every day with placebos.

In fact, in some European countries, the mother will actually eat the placebo after the baby is born. And she usually feels much better for no medical reason.

So here's what you do with your bad medical school grades," I said. "Ignore them."

That young man did exactly that.

And just six weeks later, he was expelled.

He took up calligraphy.

He's now very happy as a practising doctor—with some very nice looking diplomas.

I'm told he's helped put an end to a lot of people's suffering.

Vaguen picks up the glass of water and places it behind the table where it cannot be seen by the audience.

Picture a glass of water.

A different glass of water.

> Now drink one half of it, and pour the other half out of a window.
>
> Now take the glass and wash it.
>
> Now dry it.
>
> Hold it up and check your handiwork.
>
> Don't drop it!

He flinches slightly.

> Is it clean?
>
> Good.
>
> Now put it away.
>
> In the cupboard where the glasses go.

Vaguen says nothing, simply smiling as he returns the glass of water to the table-top. Perhaps he's thinking of how the audience will view the glasses of water in their own lives differently now, thanks to what he's just told them. Perhaps he's not.

> Now along your path to infinite Ignorance there will be nay-sayers—those wicked men who say "Nay! Your philosophy is absurd, and now I'll try to corner you with logic, reason, and sense."
>
> To overcome this, we can look back to prehistoric history.
>
> We all remember the story of O-edipus and the Spinx, who asked him three riddles, namely:
>
> "Why do you look so much like your wife?"
>
> "Remember that guy you killed that time—the one in the crown—didn't he look like you too, only older?"
>
> And
>
> "How come your kids can't walk in a straight line or uncross their eyes?"

As we know, O-edipus successfully answered these questions and went on to become king of Egypt.

And in the same way the Riddles of Ignorance can be your own personal pyramids: great, heavy blocks of stone that defy logic, reason and understanding.

So here they are, the three Riddles of Ignorance, in alphabetical order.

Riddle A

A man is staring into a mirror.

Looking at the man he sees in the mirror, he says

"Brothers and sisters I have none, but that man there is my father's son."

Who is he looking at?

Vaguen solicits guesses from the audience at this point, but for some reason the correct guess has never yet been given.

Some people occasionally suggest the answer "himself."

Vaguen dispenses with these misguided ig-students politely but efficiently.

I'll tell you.

He's looking at Norman.

Norman!

You know, Norman?

The guy with the funny arm?

Vaguen demonstrates Norman's funny arm.

He holds his left arm straight out at the shoulder, and swings it back and forth at the elbow, like the pendulum of a grandfather clock.

You see, the man was looking in the mirror at an angle, and Norman was behind him, and a bit to the side, his funny arm going back and forth.

Only it was on the other side because of the mirror.

That's what caught the man's attention in the first place.

He was used to seeing it on this side, but he was looking in a mirror so it was on this side.

Of course, he was talking about himself—"Brothers and sisters I have none"

But he was looking at Norman.

It turned out that Norman was his brother, but the man had no idea at that time.

Norman told him about a week later, on a particularly tearful episode of Oprah.

Riddle B

Every morning, a man gets up and takes the elevator from his fifth floor apartment down to the first floor and goes to work.

Every evening he comes home, takes the elevator up to the thirtieth floor, and walks down to his fifth floor apartment.

Why?

Again, Vaguen encourages the audience to call out their guesses.

Only once has an audience-member deduced the answer successfully, and he was driven instantly mad by the joyous knowledge that his mind was so in tune with Vaguen's own.

When Vaguen has given them enough tries, he explains the answer.

It's because he's too tall to reach the fifth floor button, and he has dodgy knees, so he doesn't want to bend down.

The thirtieth floor button was the lowest one he could reach by wedging himself into the corner of the elevator.

Ah! But how does he press the first floor button in the morning?

He doesn't have to, because his friend Norman is always with him, and he'll press the first-floor button with his funny arm.

He usually gets a load of others too; they end up stopping at five floors on the way down, and have a good chat.

They often play a game to see if other people get on at all the other floors, and if they do, then Norman hasn't wasted anyone's time.

Riddle E

In the morning I go on four legs, in the afternoon, two.

At various times throughout the day, three.

The mother of my children always goes on four legs, and my mistress on two.

Her husband goes on one leg.

Who am I?

Yet again, Vaguen fields hopelessly incorrect guesses. Often, out of nowhere, someone will suggest that the answer is 'Norman'. Although why that could possibly be the case no one can explain. Finally Vaguen reveals the solution.

I'm a performing circus dog.

In the morning I go on four legs, because I'm a dog.

The show happens in the afternoon, and I'm on my two back legs, doing tricks.

At various times throughout the day, I pee—three legs.

The mother of my children is a female dog, who is not in the show, so she always goes on four legs—even when she pees.

My mistress is what we call the human woman who owns me—two legs—and her husband only has one leg.

He used to have two, but a circus tiger bit one off.

His name is Norman.

The tiger also hurt his arm.

If you understand how and why these riddles can help you, then you haven't been paying attention.

Vaguen picks up his glass, and holds it aloft.

He then sings a note so high, so pure and so true that the glass shatters in his hand, but without injuring him in the slightest. He replaces it with another glass, previously unseen behind the table.

We all have knowledge we don't want.

For some of us, that knowledge is that we know that we'll never succeed in anything we do.

Others among us will know that we're fakes—big fat British fakes.

Others still will know that we're just naughty little smarty-pant boys who will never amount to anything and who no one will ever truly love, even if they say they do.

The healthiest way to get rid of this knowledge is by burying it deep within our subconsciousnesses.

For this we need a tool that I like to call "hypnotism."

I'm going to hypnotize all of you.

Please don't worry—I'm not going to have you barking like dogs, or pretending to be babies, or dry-humping like figure-skaters.

Vaguen rolls up his jacket sleeves as he explains hypnotism.

It is quietly revealed that one sleeve of the turtleneck is missing.

I'm just going to put you all into a little trance.

While in this trance I'll reach into all of your subconsciousnesses and find a repressed memory—something you were glad to have forgotten all about.

Because it's only by remembering these things, focussing on them, and reliving them, that we can truly tamp them down, stuffing them into the furthest reaches of the Ig, and covering them with shovelfuls of Ignorance, so they won't bother us again for at least five weeks.

Now get ready to be hypnotized.

Like any good hypnotiste I've got my watch.

Vaguen takes a wrist watch out of his jacket's inner pocket.

He puts it on his left wrist, and then starts swinging his arm back and forth, not unlike Norman . . .

Focus on the watch.

You'll soon begin to feel very sleepy.

In a moment I will count to five.

At "one" you will begin to drift off the shores of consciousness.

At "two" you will begin to drift further and faster.

At "three" you will lose sight of land all . . . together . . .

Vaguen slowly falls asleep, and stands there, head slumped down.

He then wakes up with a start, and looks about, wide-eyed and childlike.

He speaks in a younger sounding version of his own voice.

"Where are we going, Mummy?"

He responds with an older woman's voice.

When speaking as this woman he mimes holding a steering wheel.

He alternates between the two voices, as appropriate.

"We're taking you to University. See the big buildings? That's called a campus."

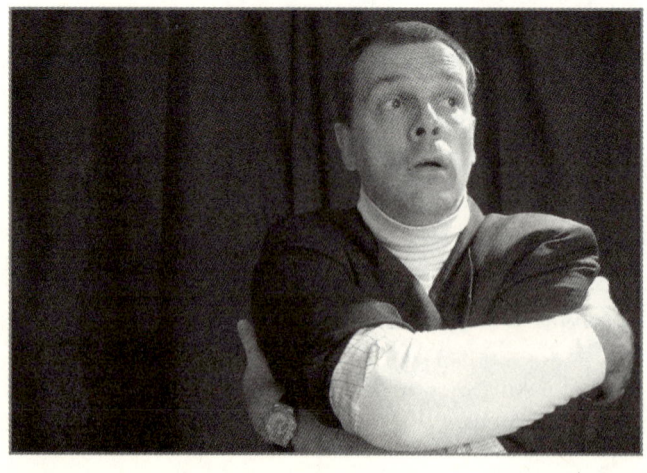

"But that sign says 'Sunnybeam Care Facility for the Mentally Inconvenient.'"

"There you go being clever again. That's just a fancy name for University."

"Who are those big men?"

"Those are the professors. See their electric teaching prods?"

"Yes."

"Now run along with the burly professors who'll help you put on your thinking jacket. I've slowed down enough. Go!"

The older woman pushes the young Vaguen out of the car.

He stands up.

His arms are pulled across his front as they're fitted into an unseen straitjacket.

"When will I see you ag—"

He makes the sound effect of a car driving off at high speed, shifting gears and disappearing in the distance.

"Oh."

Vaguen slumps his head, and then rears it up again.

This time he speaks with the voice and mannerisms of Gregory Peck.

"Seven years pass.

"Our hero has grown from a boy to a man."

He gestures to illustrate "boy" with a hand held at chest level, and "man" with his hand held an inch higher than before.

"Then, one night, he awakens to find himself surrounded by five mysterious men."

He plays the part of the man who wakes Vaguen up by poking him with his finger.

The effort of this poke raises a slight nasal grunt from this character.

Vaguen speaks as himself—newly awoken and frightened:

"Who are you? What do you want?"

He answers in a high, nasal voice.

"We ask the questions, Vaguen!

There is a slight pause.

"We don't have any questions at this time.

"And now, because I was going to anyway, I will tell you who we are and what we want.

"We are the Ignorati—the five most Ignorant men in the world.

"We aspire to be the secret rulers of this planet.

"My name is Norman.

"Vaguen, we Ignorati believe in a lesser being—an inferior intelligence, that can see some of our thoughts and certain actions and events that take place around the world some of the time, if the weather's clear.

"Depending on what's on the news.

"This part-knowing, part-loving, semi-powerful being we call 'dog'.

"Dog is un-nipotent.

"Dog is semi-scient.

"Dog is some-nipresent.

"Beware of dog, Vaguen.

> "*Beware of dog.*
>
> "Vaguen, you have been chosen.
>
> "You will do our bidding, and spread Ignorance to the world.
>
> "In order for us to rule, the world must be Ignorant.
>
> "Otherwise, it's too hard.
>
> "We have spent several hours creating a plan for you.
>
> "It's fool-proof!
>
> ". . . or at least fool-resistant!"

Norman laughs heartily at his own joke, which dies a painful death.

His laughter tapers off as he realizes he's the only one laughing.

> "You will spread our message using the medium that reaches the most people: *theatre.*
>
> "And you will do it in the most influential country in the world: *Canada.*
>
> "You will go to the most important city in Canada—*and then* you will go to Edmonton (or whichever city the show is being done in)—the best darn city in Canada.
>
> "And the least susceptible to flattery.
>
> "You will push Ignorance as a philosophy of some kind.
>
> "And we will rule some of the world!"

Norman peals off a cackling evil laugh which ends with a Scooby-Doo laugh.

All the while he tries to pound his fist into the palm of his other hand, but keeps missing.

He eventually succeeds.

"Remember . . . if you succeed in making only one person Ignorant . . . that's nowhere near enough . . .

"We need at least . . . well aim for ten get five, that's okay.

"Now we will hypnotize you."

Norman starts swinging his left arm back and forth, like the pendulum on a grandfather clock.

"Look at the watch, Vaguen.

"Look at it go back and forth.

"Back and forth . . ."

Norman falls asleep, and then wakes up with a start.

He speaks in an even higher pitched and more nasal voice.

"Wake up, Norman!"

"Who are you?"

"We ask the questions, Norman.

"We don't have any questions at this time. We are the even older Ignorati, and someday you will be an Ignorati after us!"

Norman recovers.

"Whoa, whoa—what happened there?

"I hypnotized myself there!

"How embarrassing.

"Be careful of that, Vaguen—that can happen sometimes. It's easier than you think . . ."

He resumes swinging his arm, this time using his right hand to shield his eyes from the allure of the shiny watch as it swings back and forth . . . back and forth . . .

back . . . and . . . fo— "who are you?" "We ask the questions! We don't have any questions at this time. One day, you will be asked to insert stage directions in a script of a "comedy show." This you will do free of charge, and you will describe the goings-on with a reverence that covers up the flaws and holes in the philosophy and performance. Now, back to work."

Norman speaks again.

> "Watch the watch, Vaguen!
>
> "You will do our bidding subconsciously.
>
> "When I snap my fingers you will wake up and remember none of this.
>
> "Except what we want you to remember.
>
> "You know fellas; I think that's what went wrong all those other times.
>
> "I bet this one works, now that we've added that caveat. Is it a caveat? Or a provis—"

He snaps his fingers.

Vaguen snaps out of his elaborate flashback instantly.

> Now to you, no time has passed.
>
> But don't you feel like a great heavy weight has been pushed deep down through your shoulders?
>
> I know I do.
>
> Now, I hope by this point I've shown you that Ignorance is a good and useful thing.
>
> And let me tell you, you're about to embark on a wonderful journey.
>
> You now have the tools to make Ignorance the extinguished lighthouse in the fog of your day-to-day existence.

You have the Igmantra.

You're familiar with tools to return to Ignorant breathing.

You can use the Riddles of Ignorance to cloud your own and other people's minds.

Now some of you may be scientists, scholars, gym teachers, or from any of a dozen other jobs that require intelligence and education.

You may worry that this hinders you on the path to infinite Ignorance.

And yes it does. You are further back on the road, but you're here. And that means you're facing the right way.

If you will, you could take inspiration from my own story.

I myself have had to overcome many obstacles on the way to being as Ignorant as I am.

I was an intelligent child.

I came from a happy home.

Vaguen twitches at this statement.

My parents loved me and supported me in everything I did.

Twitch

Especially my mother.

Twitch

She was always commenting on how clever I was.

In many ways it was my mother who set me on the path to Ignorance all those years ago.

I'll never forget the day I came home from my first day at school, with a huge smile on my face, saying

"Mummy, mummy, you were wrong!

"All the other kids liked me and I made loads of new friends!"

My mother said,

"If the other kids liked you it's only because they don't know you.

"Once they get to know you, which they will after I've made a few phone calls, they'll treat you with the fear and disdain that you deserve."

Soon after that I went to University.

I was enrolled quite young. I didn't want to go at first, but my parents told me:

"If you love someone set them free. If they love you, they'll untie themselves from the rock and swim back to the surface.

"Like your puppy didn't.

"I guess he didn't really love you."

I studied at the Sunnybeam University for the Mentally Intelligent.

Twitch!

I had a great time.

Made a lot of friends—crazy friends!

You only meet people like that in college.

I still remember the pillow fights I'd have with this one big guy . . .

Vaguen mimes a pillow being held over his own face with determination.

Like anyone I experimented a bit with drugs.

Strange, in my school, it wasn't really frowned on by the professors.

It was positively encouraged.

Sometimes you even felt pressured. In a knee on the chest strapped to the bed kind of way.

But don't think I didn't work hard.

I must have woven at least fifteen baskets.

I studied a bit of this and that

Arts & crafts

Electricity

Twitch!!

Maze theory, I liked.

But my favourite was Art History.

I could stare for hours at the paintings of Rorschach.

He did some wonderful nudes.

Of my mother.

Being stabbed.

To death!

Over and over.

With a broken wooden spoon.

Who's a smarty-pants now??

HA HA HA HA!

Duh . . .

Duh . . .

Duh . . .

Then one morning I woke up.

I realized that knowledge wasn't giving me the happiness I wanted.

Knowledge isn't good.

It's bad.

Knowledge is power.

Power corrupts.

Absolute power corrupts too.

Perhaps even more than regular power . . .

So I began to formulate some of the ideas I've presented you with today.

Over the strenuous objections of my professors I dropped out of university.

I started touring and doing seminars.

And I've seen Ignorance help a lot of people.

But not everyone.

Some reject it, like a body rejecting a pig's lung.

But even those *filthy smarty-pantses* can all agree on the one thing we all agree on—

What you don't know can't hurt you.

Therefore, the man who knows nothing . . . is invincible.

Ignorance can protect you from everything.

An Igmaster cannot even be hurt by physical things.

> Like emotional problems.
>
> Like the fact that MY MOTHER HATED MY GUTS!
>
> AHHHHHHHHHH!!
>
> Duh . . .
>
> Uh oh!!!
>
> I'm very sorry!
>
> Duh!

In a cruel Scottish accent:

> "Here come the child catchers and it's off to the peach mines with you my lad!"
>
> Duh . . .

Singing and dancing:

> You take the high road and I'll kick your teeth in . . .

He splashes himself in the face with his glass of water.

He seems to have recovered himself.

> Ladies and Gentlemen, this glass of water, delivered directly into the brain via the nostrils, has won me a temporary reprieve.

He looks at the front row.

> And I think some of you, too.
>
> As you can see, sometimes "Duh" is not enough.
>
> Sometimes over-abundant knowledge, or a concrete certainty of . . . your own inadequacy, for instance,
>
> Or how much you hate the taste of cabbage,

> Or the feeling of water up your nose,
>
> Or why she gave me the yummiest stew I ever had but didn't tell me why I never saw Fluffy again,
>
> . . . proves to be "Duh-proof"
>
> Or at least . . . "Duh-resistant"!

Vaguen smiles hopefully as this joke dies a painful death.

> In these situations there's only one option left:
>
> The last resort
>
> The Ultimate Weapon of Ignorance.

Vaguen consummates the suspense of the cloth covering the object on the table by whipping off the cloth in one swift movement.

Beneath the cloth is revealed: another black cloth covering whatever's under there.

It isn't quite clear what is under there.

Because there's the second black cloth on it.

He holds up the first black cloth and returns to centre stage with it.

> This cloth is the Ultimate Weapon of Ignorance.
>
> Watch carefully.

Vaguen drapes the cloth over his head, and then stands there.

> Oh yes.
>
> That is nice.
>
> I am so happy.
>
> I see no wet stage and angry theatre technician.

I see no empty seats.

He sighs.

He removes the cloth.

But sometimes even the Ultimate Weapon doesn't work.

Because even though I restrict one sense—vi-zhee-on—I still receive information through the other three.

So we need something better.

We need . . . the *Pen*ultimate Weapon of Ignorance!!

Vaguen whips off the other black cloth and reveals . . .

A piece of pine board, a full one inch thick, suspended over the space between two piles of bricks.

He holds up the wood in one hand and knocks it with the knuckles of his other hand to illustrate its solidity.

This wood represents a solid wooden barrier suspended on two piles of bricks.

Above is where we are—The Land of Knowing Too Much.

Underneath is where we want to be: The Land of Ignorance.

The land of safety.

The land under the table.

Where mummy can't find us.

Mummy doesn't like to look under the table, because mummy has a bad back.

"You made mummy's back hurt."

"No I didn't!"

"Yes you did, with your big head."

"I'm not listening."

"Spoon! Spoon!"

"There is no spoon!"

Vaguen splashes himself in the face with another glass of water.

He then steels himself and places his hands on either side of the bricks.

He lines up his head with the centre of the board.

It's clear he means to smash that board with his head.

Remember.

You Don't Know What Isn't Possible.

Two things you have to remember:

"You don't know what isn't possible"

And

"Whatever else happens, avoid the bricks"

That second one doesn't apply in as many situations,

But where it does apply it's very, very important.

He focuses on the feat he's about to attempt.

His concentration is plain to be seen.

You Don't Know What Isn't Possible.

You Don't Know What Isn't Possible.

You Don't Know

What Isn't

Possible . . .

Vaguen smashes with the board with his head.

The board breaks cleanly in two.

The audience yelps in wonder.

Vaguen stands up, unharmed, smiling confidently.

He holds his fingers in a steeple position.

There is wild applause and admiration.

Vaguen goes to walk back to centre stage and falls down, unconscious, flat on his back.

There is a pause as Vaguen lies on the stage.

This pause lasts longer than the audience expects it's going to.

Vaguen doesn't get up.

Soon, Vaguen's own voice is heard from the sound system.

> Ladies and Gentlemen, if you're listening to this recording then it's happened again.
>
> I have crashed through the wooden barrier of knowledge and reached another state of consciousness—a lower state of consciousness.
>
> A state I like to call "un."
>
> Please do not be alarmed.
>
> The failsafe system to which you are listening has been specifically designed for this exact situation.
>
> I would ask you to please refrain from touching Vaguen while we continue with the seminar.

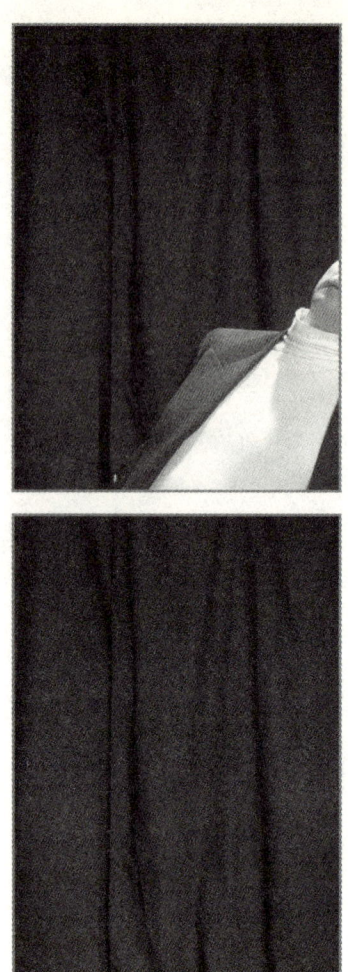

The recorded voice clears his throat.

    From Ignorance comes Happiness.

    From Ignorance comes Confidence.

    Ignorance is Limitless Possibilities.

    Know your limits,

        and Ignore what you know.

Walk with me now down the Boulevard of Confusion.

There you will find the Gateway to Naiveté.

Go through that gate.

On the other side you will find the Path of Befuddlement.

Follow it.

It will lead you to the Double Doors of Uncertainty.

Walk through the left one.

You will find yourself in the Corridor of Question Marks.

At the fourth door on the right, stop.

Knock twice short and once long, then enter.

You will be standing in the Rumpus Room of Endarkenment.

Climb through the window in the north wall.

You will drop fifty feet to the Sidewalk of Unanswerability.

Drag yourself down that sidewalk to the Corner of Bafflement.

There you will find the Boulevard of Confusion

And beyond that, who knows?

No one.

The lights fade to black.

The audience applauds.

The lights come up for curtain call, but Vaguen is still lying unconscious on the stage.

The lights come up and down like they do in a regular curtain call anyway.

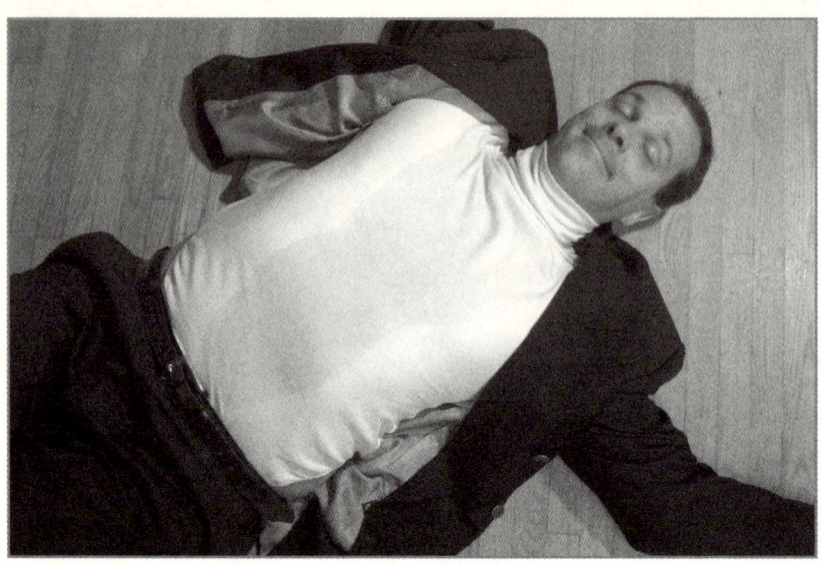

Vaguen doesn't move.

House lights come up, and mystical mysterious music plays, as the audience gets up, not entirely sure whether to leave or not.

Every five to ten seconds the music is interrupted by Vaguen's own recorded voice, saying:

> Please refrain from touching Vaguen as you leave the theatre.
>
> Please refrain from touching Vaguen as you leave the theatre.
>
> Please refrain from touching Vaguen as you LEAVE THE THEATRE!
>
> As you leave the theatre, which you should be doing now, please refrain from touching Vaguen.
>
> Please, don't touch Vaguen, as you leave the theatre.
>
> Please keep your hands off Vaguen's person as you leave the theatre.
>
> Please refrain from touching Vaguen as you leave the theatre, and go about your lives.

As you, LEAVE THE THEATRE! please, don't touch Vaguen.

A sleeping Vaguen is a happy Vaguen. Please leave the theatre quietly...AND QUICKLY!

The technician comes on, with mop and bucket, starts to mop up water

He or she moves Vaguen's legs out of the way, before realizing that it would be easier to drag the whole body out of the way.

He or she then drags Vaguen off by one foot and then returns and finishes mopping up.

The recorded prompts continue:

You've all got homes to go to, move along, nothing to see here.

Don't you need to go to the bathroom, right now?

Get out! I mean it! Thank you.

The remaining audience members are shuffled out the door by the theatre staff.

A Note On The Penultimate Weapon Of Ignorance

My favourite thing to hear when I meet someone who's seen 'The Power of Ignorance' in performance is "Chris! You're hilarious/brilliant/a genius! I have my own TV station/movie studio/publishing company! And I'd love to make 'The Power of Ignorance' into our next hit show/blockbuster/tax write-off!"

But my second-favourite thing to hear is, "You know, you might want to be more careful. I could totally see where you had cut the board."

When TJ and I decided that Vaguen should finish the show by smashing his head through an inch-thick piece of pine we spent a great deal of time trying to come up with an elaborate ploy to make it look real. We settled on a plan involving misdirection and double-bluff to substitute a pre-cut board. That substitution would definitely have been the most intricate and difficult thing I had ever done on stage.

It turns out it's just a lot easier to really do it.

The nice thing is, the joke works whether the audience have convinced themselves it's fake or not. And, as I found out one very painful afternoon in Edmonton, it also works if I have to hit the wood a couple of times before it breaks.

The handspring, however, is completely fake, and the hi-tech pulleys and seventeen burly stagehands required to pull it off make up a full eighty-five percent of the production budget.

Acknowledgements

Special thanks to . . .

Jeff Sumerel and Sam Reynolds.

Lisa Pijuan-Nomura, organizer of the RED Cabaret series, where the first snippet of the play was performed. Since then Lisa has included the show in the RED festival and produced several one-off performances.

Aviva Armour-Ostroff, curator of Lab Cab, another testing ground for Vaguen's early appearances.

And . . . Alana Eve Burman, Chuck McEwen, Bridget MacIntosh, Jeremy Hechtman, Patrick Goddard, Nick Kowalchuk, Bertram Schneider, Miki Stricker. All of our various technicians. Mike Rinaldi, Rick Kunst, Bruce Horak, Andrew Sanger, Kelly Finnegan, Mark Jackson, Albie Hewlett for the Rivers in Portugal line. And Mrs. Nicole Barnett.

Afterword

by TJ Dawe

For anyone who's interested, here's how it all happened.

The script came to me in a dream, and I wrote it all in one sitting. That Gibbs is nothing but a puppet.

It's an elaborate reworking of something I once read in a fortune cookie.

It's a reaction to the growing number of self-help gurus, and how many people flock to them, willing to pay anything and everything for The Answer. What's wrong with those idiots?? They should listen to ME!!!

It's stolen. There's a guy who tours one-man shows in Borneo doing the original version. I don't think he knows about us doing it. Don't tell him.

Chris improvised all of this for me while sitting on the couch at a potluck supper. I went home and transcribed it from memory. I presented it to him the next day, and he didn't remember having said any of it. He still doesn't. I give him co-writing credit all the same.

It's a somewhat disguised retelling of the Oedipus myth. The notes for the show were found scribbled in pencil in the margins of a book of Greek mythology I got from a used book store.

The concept was conceived of while drunk for six weeks, the writing was done stoned over three weeks, and then it was rehearsed underground, in a room with mud walls, lit by a single candle, for one day, whilst over-eating.

I was doing a festival in Charleston, South Carolina. There was a show in my venue called *Kudzula*. I went and saw it. The gist of it was a guy on stage, dubbing all the voices for the low-budget monster movie he'd just made (being projected on the screen next to him), trying to impress the Hollywood bigwig sitting in the audience, waiting to use the editing suite next. It was very funny, and equally bizarre. The guy doing it had a beautifully original humour. As part of the show he played a few minutes of a short film he'd made, just to warm up the projector. The short was called *The Power of Ignorance*. It was the same actor, dressed in a turtleneck, suit jacket, and wearing a medallion, looking at the camera with hypnotic confidence, encouraging you to release your hold on knowledge, and join him in the ignorance mantra: "*Duh.*" He said the igmantra with determination, and seriousness. He meant it. "*Duh.*" It sounded like the truth. It sounded stupid. He said it again and again. I'd never seen anything so funny.

A month and a half later I was doing the Winnipeg Fringe. I'd just seen Chris Gibbs' solo show *Gibberish*, and loved it. Got talking to him afterwards. "We should write something together" I said. "Righty-ho, pip pip, cheerio and all that!" he said—or something to that effect. He's British. He'd just moved to Toronto. I lived in Toronto. Our places were walking distance from each other. "But what will we write about?" said he. "Well there's this short film I saw part of in South Carolina," said me.

The people at my Charleston venue put me in contact with the guy. His name was Jeff Sumerel. He's a filmmaker, based out of Greenville, SC. I emailed him. Told him what I wanted to do. He liked it. He'd wanted to do a longer, stage version of the show when he'd done the film ten years before, but had never found a venue. It wouldn't work in a comedy club. You'd need a theatre kind of setting, but not a traditional theatre. Somewhere where you can blend genres. Where you can do strange things. Where you can take the audience to strange places and have them happily come along. The Fringe!

Jeff sent me the ten-minute video. Chris and I watched it—this infomercial of a guy preaching the virtues of ignorance over knowledge. As it finished, Chris said "I'm flattered that when you saw this, the first person that came to mind was me."

Chris and I wrote the script over the next six months, off and on. It opened at the Montreal Fringe on Friday the 13th. Of June. 2003. The audience was frighteningly silent. The next day was better. The day after that was fantastic. Then Toronto wasn't so good. Chris changed a few things. It really hit its stride in Winnipeg. In Edmonton, people lined up for hours and hours for it every time. It grew as it toured the Fringe circuit. And then it grew some more outside the Fringe circuit. It's up to ninety minutes now. And it's still growing. And now there's going to be a book to sell. Not just the script—a self-help book. I'll give you a sales pitch for that in a few paragraphs.

Chris's background includes stand-up comedy, improv theatre and street performing—all three of which demand that the performer smash the fourth wall and deal with anything and everything that happens, as it happens. I saw him do this many times. In Edmonton, someone in a hallway near the theatre dropped something that made a loud clattering sound. Chris wove it right in. "Stop, focus and breathe," was the line. Chris made it "Stop . . . focus . . . put down anything you're carrying . . . any large metal tray . . . put it down loudly or quietly, it doesn't matter . . . completely ignoring the 'Quiet Please, Show in Progress' signs set up all around you . . ."

Another time a guy got up from the front and centre to go to the washroom. Chris dealt with him in character, again, working it right into what was happening in the plot at that point. He spoke as Norman, head of the Ignorati, breaking off his instructions to Vaguen with a warning—"And one day, Vaguen, you will meet your nemesis. A man named . . . Little Neddie Tinybladder. Whose crouched-over posture doesn't give him the invisibility he thinks it does." The man, at that point, stayed where he was, three-quarters of the way through the audience. He turned and looked back at the stage. Chris kept ad libbing. The audience laughed. The man didn't move.

He was wearing a white golf shirt and had a big bald head. He was very visible. Chris ended up adding ten minutes to the show.

In Coquitlam, BC, he asked for possible answers for the third absurd and impossible riddle of ignorance: "In the morning I go on four legs. In the afternoon, two. Several times throughout the day, three. The mother of my children always goes on four legs. My mistress goes on two, and her husband on one. Who am I?" A man volunteered the equally cryptic and absurd suggestion "the ouzo vendor." "Pardon?" asked Chris, in character. "The ouzo vendor," the man said, already starting to laugh. "Ah." said Chris "The ouzo vendor. I initially thought you'd said 'The Ussel-vander.' And 'The Ussel-vander' would have made less sense than 'the ouzo vendor.' But only slightly." Chris kept going with this, and the man had tears of laughter coming down his face. That man was my dad.

I'd like to thank Jeff Sumerel and Sam Reynolds (Sam came up with the concept in the first place, and played the disciple Ed Ray Monsoon in the ten-minute film) for their total generosity in letting us extrapolate this idea of theirs. Some of the lines in the stage show come directly from that short film. Most are variations, or new directions Chris and I took it in. But either way, Sam and Jeff were always supportive and respectful, and allowed us great freedom. And that's not that easy to do. Much less with someone you've never actually met. Sam also set up a virtual office so that the four of us could maintain communication throughout the writing and working of the *Power of Ignorance* self-help book (entitled *The Power of Ignorance: 14 Steps to Using Your Ignorance*) (which contains very little material from the stage show—it's almost all new stuff) (Published by Brindle & Glass) (and for sale wherever you're getting this from, that's for sure). Great thanks for all their help over both projects.

You can see some of Jeff Sumerel's work at www.spontaneous.net.

TJ DAWE, winner of the Just For Laughs Comedy Award, is the author of *The Slip-Knot* and *Labrador* (Brindle & Glass), as well as seemingly hundreds of other successful Fringe plays. He lives near Vancouver, but not too near.

Born in England, CHRIS "HILARIOUS" GIBBS first came to Canada as one half of the comedy duo HOOPAL. He moved to Canada in 2002 and has since toured three one-man shows, *Gibberish*, *The Power of Ignorance* and *Antoine Feval*. He lives in Toronto.